Hy

The Art of Cozy

Introduction: Defining Hygge and its Origins

Hygge (pronounced "hoo-gah") is a Danish term that has gained popularity worldwide in recent years. It is a concept that is difficult to translate into other languages, but is often described as a feeling of coziness, warmth, and contentment. In essence, it's about creating a comfortable and inviting atmosphere, where people can relax and enjoy the simple pleasures in life.

The origins of hygge can be traced back to Denmark, where it has been a part of the country's culture for centuries. The word itself is believed to come from the Norwegian word "hygge," which means "to comfort" or "to console." It was first used in Danish writing in the 19th century, and has since become an integral part of Danish life.

Hygge is often associated with winter and the colder months, when Danes spend more time indoors. However, it can also be enjoyed throughout the year. The key to hygge is creating an environment that feels warm and inviting, whether that's through lighting, decor, or spending time with loved ones.

Hygge is not just about the physical environment, however. It's also about the mindset and approach to life. Danes place a strong emphasis on enjoying life's simple pleasures, such as spending time with family and friends, enjoying a cup of coffee, or reading a good book. They also prioritize self-care and taking time to relax and recharge.

One of the reasons hygge has become so popular in recent years is that it offers a way to combat the stress and busyness of modern life. In a world where people are constantly connected and always on the go, hygge offers a chance to slow down and enjoy the moment.

In this book, we will explore the many facets of hygge, from creating cozy spaces to enjoying simple pleasures and embracing a slower pace of life. We will look at the history and origins of hygge, as well as how it has evolved over time. We will also offer practical tips and advice for incorporating hygge into your own life, whether that's through your home decor, your approach to self-care, or your relationships with others.

Ultimately, hygge is about finding joy and contentment in the present moment. It's about creating a sense of warmth and comfort in your surroundings, and cultivating a mindset of gratitude and appreciation for the simple things in life. In the following chapters, we will explore how you can embrace hygge and make it a part of your own life.

Understanding the Danish Culture and its Connection to Hygge

To truly understand hygge, it's important to look at the culture from which it originated: Denmark. Denmark consistently ranks as one of the happiest countries in the world, and many people believe that hygge is a key reason for this. But what is it about Danish culture that makes it so conducive to this sense of comfort and contentment?

One of the key aspects of Danish culture is the concept of "janteloven," which translates to "the law of Jante." This refers to a set of social norms that prioritize humility, equality, and community over individual success or achievement. This can be seen in many aspects of Danish life, from their education system (which emphasizes collaboration over competition) to their approach to work (which prioritizes work-life balance and equal opportunities).

Another important aspect of Danish culture is their love of simplicity and minimalism. Danes are known for their clean and minimalist design aesthetic, which is reflected in everything from their home decor to their fashion choices. This love of simplicity is also reflected in their approach to food, which often focuses on fresh, seasonal ingredients prepared simply and with care.

Despite their love of simplicity, Danes also place a high value on quality and craftsmanship. This can be seen in their design and fashion industries, which prioritize quality materials and expert craftsmanship. This emphasis on quality over quantity is also reflected in their approach to socializing, which often involves spending quality time with a small group of close friends or family members.

All of these aspects of Danish culture contribute to the sense of comfort and contentment that is central to hygge. By prioritizing community, simplicity, and quality, Danes are able to create an environment that feels warm and inviting, even during the cold and dark winter months.

In addition to these cultural factors, the Danish climate also plays a role in the development of hygge. Denmark experiences long, dark winters with very little daylight. As a result, Danes have learned to create a sense of warmth and coziness in their homes and in their relationships with others.

Overall, the connection between hygge and Danish culture is a complex one. It involves a combination of social norms, design aesthetics, and climate-related factors, all of which contribute to a sense of comfort and contentment that is central to Danish life. By understanding these cultural factors, we can gain a deeper appreciation for the importance of hygge and learn how to incorporate it into our own lives.

Hygge and the Importance of Creating Cozy Spaces

One of the most important aspects of hygge is creating a warm and inviting atmosphere, whether in your home or in other spaces. By cultivating a sense of comfort and coziness, you can create an environment that is conducive to relaxation and enjoyment. In this chapter, we will explore the importance of creating cozy spaces and offer practical tips for doing so.

First and foremost, creating a cozy space is about paying attention to the details. This might include things like lighting, textiles, and decor. When it comes to lighting, for example, soft and warm lighting is key. This might involve using table lamps or candles instead of harsh overhead lighting. Similarly, incorporating soft textiles like blankets and pillows can help create a sense of warmth and comfort.

In terms of decor, creating a cozy space often involves incorporating natural materials like wood and stone. This might involve adding a wooden coffee table or incorporating natural stone accents in your decor. These materials can help create a sense of warmth and connection to nature, which is important for creating a cozy atmosphere.

Another important aspect of creating cozy spaces is incorporating personal touches. This might involve displaying family photos or artwork that holds personal meaning. By surrounding yourself with things that bring you joy and comfort, you can create a space that feels uniquely your own.

When it comes to creating cozy spaces, it's also important to consider the layout and flow of the space. Creating a comfortable seating area that encourages conversation and connection is key. This might involve rearranging furniture or adding seating options like floor cushions or beanbag chairs.

In addition to creating cozy spaces in your home, it's also important to think about other spaces where you spend time. For example, creating a cozy workspace can help you feel more comfortable and productive. This might involve adding soft lighting or incorporating personal touches like plants or photos.

Overall, creating cozy spaces is an important part of cultivating hygge in your life. By paying attention to the details, incorporating personal touches, and creating comfortable seating areas, you can create an environment that is warm and inviting. Whether you're spending time at home or in other spaces, creating a sense of comfort and coziness is key to enjoying the simple pleasures of life.

Finding Joy in Simplicity: Hygge in Minimalism

In recent years, minimalism has become a popular trend in home decor and lifestyle choices. At its core, minimalism is about simplifying your life and focusing on the things that truly matter. In many ways, this philosophy aligns with the principles of hygge. In this chapter, we will explore the connection between hygge and minimalism and offer tips for incorporating both into your life.

At its core, hygge is about finding joy and contentment in the simple pleasures of life. This might involve spending time with loved ones, enjoying a cup of coffee, or simply reading a good book. Similarly, minimalism is about paring down your possessions and focusing on the essentials. By eliminating clutter and excess, you can create a sense of calm and clarity in your life.

One of the key principles of minimalism is that less is more. This is also true in the context of hygge. By focusing on a few key elements, such as warm lighting and soft textiles, you can create a cozy and inviting atmosphere without overwhelming the senses. This might involve incorporating natural materials like wood and stone, or opting for a neutral color palette that creates a sense of calm.

Another way that minimalism and hygge overlap is in their emphasis on quality over quantity. When it comes to decorating your home or choosing possessions, both philosophies prioritize investing in high-quality items that will last for years. This might involve investing in a well-made piece of furniture or choosing to buy clothes that are well-constructed and timeless in style.

In addition to simplifying your possessions, both hygge and minimalism also prioritize simplifying your schedule. This might involve saying no to activities or commitments that don't align with your priorities, or simply carving out time for relaxation and self-care.

Ultimately, the connection between hygge and minimalism is about finding joy in simplicity. By focusing on the things that truly matter and eliminating excess, you can create a sense of peace and contentment in your life. Whether you're incorporating hygge into your home decor or adopting a minimalist lifestyle, the key is to find the balance that works for you and brings you joy.

Hygge and the Art of Relaxation: Creating a Calming Atmosphere

One of the key principles of hygge is creating a warm and inviting atmosphere that promotes relaxation and calm. In this chapter, we will explore the connection between hygge and relaxation and offer practical tips for creating a calming atmosphere in your home and in your life.

One of the most important aspects of creating a calming atmosphere is paying attention to your senses. This might involve incorporating soft and warm lighting, playing calming music or nature sounds, or using aromatherapy to create a relaxing scent. Essential oils like lavender, chamomile, and ylang-ylang are all known for their calming properties and can be used in a diffuser or added to a warm bath.

Another important aspect of creating a calming atmosphere is incorporating natural elements. This might involve bringing plants into your space, incorporating natural materials like wood or stone, or simply opening your windows to let in fresh air and natural light. By connecting with nature, you can create a sense of peace and tranquility in your space.

In addition to creating a calming atmosphere in your physical space, it's also important to prioritize relaxation and self-care in your daily routine. This might involve taking a warm bath with soothing salts or oils, practicing meditation or yoga, or simply taking a few moments each day to sit quietly and breathe deeply. By prioritizing relaxation and self-care, you can create a sense of calm and well-being in your life.

Another way to promote relaxation and calm is to minimize distractions and interruptions. This might involve turning off your phone or computer during designated relaxation times, or simply setting boundaries with friends or family members to ensure that you have the space and time you need to unwind.

Ultimately, creating a calming atmosphere is about finding what works best for you and prioritizing relaxation and self-care in your life. By paying attention to your senses, incorporating natural elements, and minimizing distractions, you can create a space that promotes peace and tranquility. Whether you're practicing hygge in your home decor or simply looking to add more relaxation to your daily routine, the key is to find what brings you joy and contentment.

Hygge at Home: Decorating and Designing for Comfort and Coziness

One of the key ways to embrace hygge in your life is through your home decor and design choices. Creating a warm and inviting atmosphere can help promote relaxation and contentment, whether you're spending time alone or with loved ones. In this chapter, we will explore the principles of hygge in home decor and offer practical tips for creating a cozy and inviting space.

One of the most important aspects of hygge in home decor is creating a sense of warmth and comfort. This might involve incorporating soft textiles like blankets and pillows, using warm lighting, or adding natural elements like wood or stone. Soft, neutral color palettes can also create a sense of calm and tranquility.

Another important aspect of hygge in home decor is incorporating personal touches. This might involve displaying family photos, incorporating artwork that holds personal meaning, or simply surrounding yourself with things that bring you joy and comfort.

When it comes to furniture and layout, creating a cozy and inviting space often involves incorporating comfortable seating options like oversized chairs or sofas, or adding floor cushions for a more casual seating option. The layout of your space should encourage conversation and connection, with seating arranged in a way that feels welcoming and inclusive.

In addition to creating a cozy atmosphere, it's also important to prioritize functionality and organization in your home decor choices. This might involve choosing furniture pieces that are both beautiful and practical, or incorporating storage solutions that keep clutter at bay.

Ultimately, the key to embracing hygge in home decor is finding a balance between comfort and functionality, while also incorporating personal touches that make your space uniquely your own. By paying attention to the details, incorporating soft textiles and warm lighting, and creating a sense of warmth and comfort, you can create a space that promotes relaxation and contentment. Whether you're looking to transform your entire home or simply create a cozy corner to relax in, the principles of hygge can guide your design choices and help you create a space that brings you joy and comfort.

Hygge and Food: Cooking and Dining with Friends and Family

In addition to creating a warm and inviting atmosphere in your home, hygge also emphasizes the importance of food and drink in fostering a sense of community and togetherness. Whether you're enjoying a meal with friends or simply savoring a cup of coffee alone, food and drink can be a powerful tool for promoting relaxation and contentment. In this chapter, we will explore the connection between hygge and food and offer practical tips for cooking and dining with friends and family.

At its core, hygge is about finding joy and comfort in the simple pleasures of life, and food is no exception. Whether you're cooking a favorite family recipe or trying out a new dish with friends, the act of cooking and sharing a meal together can create a sense of warmth and togetherness. It's not just about the food itself, but about the experience of preparing and sharing it with others.

When it comes to cooking and dining with friends and family, hygge emphasizes the importance of creating a sense of intimacy and connection. This might involve setting a beautiful table with candles and fresh flowers, or simply dimming the lights and playing soft music to create a sense of ambiance. It's about creating an environment that feels warm and inviting, where everyone can feel comfortable and relaxed.

Another important aspect of hygge in food is the emphasis on quality over quantity. This might involve choosing fresh, seasonal ingredients and taking the time to prepare them with care. It's not about having a large quantity of food, but about savoring each bite and enjoying the experience of eating together.

In addition to cooking and dining with friends and family, hygge also emphasizes the importance of taking time for yourself to savor the simple pleasures of life. This might involve enjoying a cup of coffee or tea alone in the morning, or savoring a piece of dark chocolate as an afternoon treat. By taking time to slow down and savor these small moments, you can create a sense of contentment and peace in your daily routine.

Ultimately, the key to embracing hygge in food is to prioritize the experience of cooking and dining together, and to savor the simple pleasures of food and drink. Whether you're cooking for a crowd or enjoying a meal alone, the act of nourishing your body and soul through food and drink can create a sense of warmth and contentment that is central to hygge.

The Importance of Lighting in Creating a Hygge Atmosphere

Lighting plays a crucial role in creating a hygge atmosphere in your home. The right lighting can help create a warm and inviting space, and can promote relaxation and contentment. In this chapter, we will explore the importance of lighting in creating a hygge atmosphere and offer practical tips for incorporating lighting into your home decor.

One of the most important aspects of lighting in creating a hygge atmosphere is the color temperature. Soft, warm lighting is key to creating a cozy and inviting atmosphere. This might involve using table lamps or candles instead of harsh overhead lighting, or incorporating string lights for a subtle and warm glow.

Another important aspect of lighting in creating a hygge atmosphere is layering. By incorporating different types of lighting, you can create a sense of depth and warmth in your space. This might involve using a combination of table lamps, floor lamps, and overhead lighting to create a variety of lighting options. Dimmer switches can also be helpful in creating a cozy atmosphere, allowing you to adjust the lighting to your preference.

In addition to incorporating soft and warm lighting, it's also important to consider the placement of your lighting sources. For example, incorporating lighting sources at varying heights can help create a sense of depth and visual interest in your space. Placing table lamps on different surfaces, such as a coffee table or side table, can also create a sense of balance and harmony in your lighting.

Another way to incorporate lighting into your hygge decor is by using candles. Candles not only provide soft and warm lighting, but they also add a cozy and inviting fragrance to your space. Scented candles with warm and comforting fragrances like vanilla or cinnamon can help create a sense of comfort and relaxation.

Ultimately, the key to incorporating lighting into your hygge decor is to create a warm and inviting atmosphere that promotes relaxation and contentment. By incorporating soft and warm lighting, layering lighting sources, and considering the placement of your lighting sources, you can create a space that feels cozy and inviting. Whether you're reading a book, enjoying a cup of tea, or simply spending time with loved ones, the right lighting can help create a sense of warmth and togetherness that is central to hygge.

Creating a Hygge Lifestyle: Mindful Living and Gratitude

Hygge is more than just a decorating trend or lifestyle choice – it's a way of life that emphasizes the importance of mindfulness and gratitude. In this chapter, we will explore the principles of hygge in creating a mindful and grateful lifestyle, and offer practical tips for incorporating these principles into your daily routine.

At its core, hygge is about finding joy and contentment in the simple pleasures of life, and mindfulness is key to achieving this. Mindfulness involves being present in the moment and paying attention to your thoughts and feelings without judgment. By practicing mindfulness, you can learn to appreciate the small moments in life and find joy in the present moment.

One way to incorporate mindfulness into your hygge lifestyle is through the practice of meditation. Meditation involves focusing on your breath and letting go of distracting thoughts, and can help promote relaxation and mental clarity. Even just a few minutes of meditation each day can help reduce stress and increase feelings of well-being.

Another way to practice mindfulness in your daily routine is to take time to savor the simple pleasures of life. This might involve enjoying a cup of coffee in the morning without any distractions, or taking a walk outside and paying attention to the sights and sounds around you. By taking time to appreciate these small moments, you can cultivate a sense of gratitude and contentment in your daily life.

Gratitude is another key aspect of a hygge lifestyle, and involves recognizing and appreciating the good things in your life. This might involve starting a gratitude journal, where you write down a few things each day that you're grateful for. By focusing on the positive aspects of your life, you can cultivate a sense of joy and contentment that is central to hygge.

In addition to mindfulness and gratitude, a hygge lifestyle also emphasizes the importance of slowing down and simplifying your life. This might involve saying no to activities or commitments that don't align with your priorities, or simply carving out time each day for relaxation and self-care. By simplifying your life and prioritizing the things that matter most, you can create a sense of calm and well-being that is central to hygge.

Ultimately, the key to creating a hygge lifestyle is to embrace mindfulness, gratitude, and simplicity in your daily routine. By taking time to appreciate the small moments in life, practicing gratitude, and simplifying your life, you can cultivate a sense of joy and contentment that is central to the hygge philosophy. Whether you're incorporating hygge into your home decor or your daily routine, the principles of mindfulness, gratitude, and simplicity can guide your choices and help you create a life that brings you joy and contentment.

Hygge and Nature: Embracing the Outdoors

While hygge is often associated with cozy indoor spaces, it also emphasizes the importance of spending time in nature and embracing the outdoors. In fact, many aspects of hygge can be found in the natural world, from the beauty of a sunset to the warmth of a crackling fire. In this chapter, we will explore the connection between hygge and nature and offer practical tips for embracing the outdoors in your daily life.

At its core, hygge is about finding joy and contentment in the simple pleasures of life, and nature is one of the most accessible and rewarding ways to achieve this. Whether you're taking a walk in the park, spending time in your backyard, or simply looking out the window at a beautiful view, nature can help promote relaxation and well-being.

One way to incorporate nature into your hygge lifestyle is to create a comfortable outdoor space where you can relax and unwind. This might involve adding comfortable seating options like outdoor cushions or hammocks, or incorporating soft lighting like string lights or lanterns for a warm and inviting atmosphere. By creating a space that feels cozy and inviting, you can enjoy the beauty of the outdoors while still feeling comfortable and relaxed.

Another way to embrace the outdoors in your hygge lifestyle is to spend time in nature on a regular basis. This might involve taking a walk in the woods, going for a hike, or simply sitting outside and enjoying the beauty of your surroundings. By taking time to appreciate the natural world, you can cultivate a sense of awe and wonder that is central to the hygge philosophy.

In addition to spending time in nature, hygge also emphasizes the importance of connecting with others in the outdoors. This might involve hosting a picnic with friends, going camping with family, or simply enjoying a bonfire with loved ones. By spending time in nature together, you can cultivate a sense of community and togetherness that is central to hygge.

Ultimately, the key to embracing the outdoors in your hygge lifestyle is to find joy and contentment in the natural world around you. Whether you're creating a comfortable outdoor space or spending time in nature on a regular basis, the principles of hygge can guide your choices and help you cultivate a sense of well-being and connection to the world around you. Whether you're enjoying the beauty of a sunset or the warmth of a bonfire, the natural world has much to offer in terms of comfort, relaxation, and joy.

Hygge and Relationships: Nurturing Close Connections

At its core, hygge is about finding joy and contentment in the simple pleasures of life, and this includes the importance of nurturing close relationships with family and friends. In fact, one of the central tenets of hygge is the emphasis on togetherness and connection. In this chapter, we will explore the connection between hygge and relationships and offer practical tips for nurturing close connections in your life.

One of the key aspects of hygge in relationships is the importance of quality time spent with loved ones. This might involve hosting a dinner party, playing board games with friends, or simply spending time chatting and catching up with family. By prioritizing these close relationships and spending quality time together, you can cultivate a sense of warmth and togetherness that is central to hygge.

Another way to nurture close relationships in your hygge lifestyle is through acts of kindness and thoughtfulness. This might involve bringing a friend their favorite coffee or surprising a loved one with a thoughtful gift. By showing love and appreciation for the people in your life, you can cultivate a sense of connection and joy that is central to the hygge philosophy.

In addition to quality time and acts of kindness, hygge also emphasizes the importance of creating a comfortable and inviting atmosphere for your loved ones. This might involve setting a beautiful table for a dinner party, or simply dimming the lights and lighting some candles to create a sense of ambiance. By creating a space that feels warm and welcoming, you can make your loved ones feel valued and cherished.

Another way to nurture close relationships in your hygge lifestyle is through the practice of forgiveness and understanding. No relationship is perfect, and it's important to cultivate a sense of compassion and empathy when conflicts arise. By practicing forgiveness and understanding, you can create a sense of connection and trust that is central to the hygge philosophy.

Ultimately, the key to nurturing close relationships in your hygge lifestyle is to prioritize quality time, show acts of kindness and thoughtfulness, create a comfortable and inviting atmosphere, and practice forgiveness and understanding. By cultivating these habits in your relationships, you can create a sense of warmth and togetherness that is central to the hygge philosophy. Whether you're spending time with family or catching up with friends, the principles of hygge can guide your choices and help you cultivate close connections that bring you joy and contentment.

The Role of Rituals and Traditions in Hygge

Hygge is about finding joy and contentment in the simple pleasures of life, and one way to achieve this is through the incorporation of rituals and traditions into your daily routine. Rituals and traditions can help create a sense of comfort and familiarity, and can promote relaxation and contentment. In this chapter, we will explore the role of rituals and traditions in hygge and offer practical tips for incorporating them into your life.

At its core, hygge is about finding joy and contentment in the present moment, and rituals and traditions can help promote mindfulness and intentionality. This might involve incorporating a morning ritual like enjoying a cup of coffee or tea in a favorite mug, or creating a bedtime routine that involves reading a book or journaling. By incorporating these rituals into your daily routine, you can create a sense of structure and intentionality that is central to the hygge philosophy.

Another way to incorporate rituals and traditions into your hygge lifestyle is through the celebration of holidays and special occasions. This might involve hosting a festive dinner party for friends and family, or simply decorating your home for the holidays. By creating a sense of celebration and festivity, you can cultivate a sense of joy and togetherness that is central to the hygge philosophy.

In addition to holidays and special occasions, hygge also emphasizes the importance of seasonal traditions and rituals. This might involve taking a walk in the woods to appreciate the changing leaves in the fall, or spending time baking holiday cookies with loved ones during the winter. By embracing the natural rhythms and changes of the seasons, you can cultivate a sense of connection and appreciation for the world around you.

Another way to incorporate rituals and traditions into your hygge lifestyle is through the practice of self-care. This might involve taking a relaxing bath with candles and soft music, or practicing a daily yoga or meditation routine. By prioritizing self-care and creating a sense of ritual around these practices, you can promote relaxation and contentment in your daily life.

Ultimately, the key to incorporating rituals and traditions into your hygge lifestyle is to find joy and contentment in the present moment. Whether you're incorporating morning or bedtime rituals, celebrating holidays and special occasions, embracing seasonal traditions, or practicing self-care, the principles of hygge can guide your choices and help you cultivate a sense of mindfulness and intentionality in your daily routine. By creating a sense of structure and familiarity, you can cultivate a sense of comfort and contentment that is central to the hygge philosophy.

Creating a Hygge Workspace: Finding Comfort in Your Job

Hygge is about finding joy and contentment in the simple pleasures of life, and this includes finding comfort and coziness in your workspace. Whether you work in an office, a cubicle, or from home, creating a hygge workspace can help promote relaxation and well-being in your job. In this chapter, we will explore the importance of creating a hygge workspace and offer practical tips for finding comfort and coziness in your job.

At its core, hygge is about finding joy and contentment in your surroundings, and this includes your workspace. Whether you're working from home or in an office, it's important to create a space that feels comfortable and inviting. This might involve adding cozy elements like a soft rug, comfortable chair, or warm lighting to create a sense of coziness.

Another way to create a hygge workspace is to personalize your surroundings with items that bring you joy and inspiration. This might involve adding photos of loved ones, artwork, or plants to your workspace to create a sense of warmth and familiarity. By surrounding yourself with items that make you happy, you can create a space that feels uniquely your own.

In addition to creating a comfortable and inviting workspace, hygge also emphasizes the importance of taking breaks and practicing self-care throughout the workday. This might involve taking a walk outside to enjoy the fresh air and sunshine, or simply taking a few minutes to stretch or meditate. By prioritizing self-care and taking breaks throughout the workday, you can promote relaxation and well-being in your job.

Another way to create a hygge workspace is to incorporate a sense of mindfulness and intentionality into your workday. This might involve creating a to-do list or prioritizing tasks to help create a sense of structure and focus. By prioritizing mindfulness and intentionality in your workday, you can create a sense of purpose and meaning in your job.

Ultimately, the key to creating a hygge workspace is to find joy and comfort in your surroundings, prioritize self-care and mindfulness, and personalize your workspace with items that bring you joy and inspiration. Whether you're working from home or in an office, the principles of hygge can guide your choices and help you create a workspace that feels comfortable, inviting, and uniquely your own. By finding comfort and coziness in your job, you can promote relaxation, well-being, and joy in your workday.

Hygge and Creativity: Embracing Arts and Crafts

Hygge is about finding joy and contentment in the simple pleasures of life, and one way to achieve this is through embracing creativity and artistic expression. Whether you're knitting a sweater, painting a picture, or learning a new craft, incorporating arts and crafts into your hygge lifestyle can promote relaxation, well-being, and a sense of accomplishment. In this chapter, we will explore the connection between hygge and creativity, and offer practical tips for incorporating arts and crafts into your life.

At its core, hygge is about finding joy and contentment in the present moment, and creativity can help promote mindfulness and intentionality. This might involve taking a break from screens and technology to embrace a tactile craft like knitting, crocheting, or woodworking. By incorporating these crafts into your daily routine, you can create a sense of structure and intentionality that is central to the hygge philosophy.

Another way to incorporate creativity into your hygge lifestyle is through the practice of journaling or creative writing. By taking the time to reflect on your thoughts and feelings, you can cultivate a sense of mindfulness and self-awareness that is central to the hygge philosophy. This might involve writing in a gratitude journal, creating poetry, or even starting a blog to share your thoughts and experiences with others.

In addition to tactile crafts and writing, hygge also emphasizes the importance of artistic expression and creative exploration. This might involve taking a painting class, trying your hand at pottery, or even learning a new musical instrument. By embracing creativity and artistic expression, you can cultivate a sense of joy and accomplishment that is central to the hygge philosophy.

Another way to incorporate creativity into your hygge lifestyle is to create a designated space for your artistic pursuits. This might involve setting up a crafting corner in your home or dedicating a space to your art supplies. By creating a space that feels inviting and comfortable, you can promote relaxation and well-being in your artistic pursuits.

Ultimately, the key to incorporating creativity into your hygge lifestyle is to find joy and contentment in the present moment. Whether you're embracing a tactile craft, writing in a journal, or exploring new artistic pursuits, the principles of hygge can guide your choices and help you cultivate a sense of mindfulness and intentionality in your creative pursuits. By prioritizing creativity and artistic expression, you can promote relaxation, well-being, and a sense of accomplishment in your hygge lifestyle.

The Role of Music and Sound in Hygge

Hygge is about finding joy and contentment in the simple pleasures of life, and one way to achieve this is through incorporating music and sound into your daily routine. Whether you're listening to your favorite songs, enjoying the sounds of nature, or simply creating a peaceful atmosphere with ambient noise, music and sound can help promote relaxation, well-being, and a sense of comfort. In this chapter, we will explore the role of music and sound in hygge, and offer practical tips for incorporating them into your life.

At its core, hygge is about finding joy and contentment in your surroundings, and music and sound can help create a sense of atmosphere and ambiance. This might involve listening to your favorite music while cooking, creating a peaceful soundscape with ambient noise, or simply enjoying the sounds of nature while taking a walk. By incorporating music and sound into your daily routine, you can create a sense of comfort and relaxation that is central to the hygge philosophy.

Another way to incorporate music and sound into your hygge lifestyle is through the practice of meditation or mindfulness. This might involve listening to calming music or guided meditations to promote relaxation and well-being, or simply taking a few moments to listen to your breath or the sounds around you. By prioritizing mindfulness and relaxation in your daily routine, you can promote a sense of calm and contentment that is central to the hygge philosophy.

In addition to promoting relaxation and well-being, music and sound can also help promote a sense of togetherness and community. This might involve hosting a sing-along or music night with friends and family, or simply enjoying a shared love of music with those around you. By creating a sense of shared enjoyment and connection through music and sound, you can promote a sense of togetherness and belonging that is central to the hygge philosophy.

Another way to incorporate music and sound into your hygge lifestyle is to create a designated space for listening and enjoying music. This might involve setting up a cozy listening corner in your home or creating a playlist of your favorite songs to enjoy throughout the day. By creating a space that feels inviting and comfortable, you can promote relaxation and well-being in your musical pursuits.

Ultimately, the key to incorporating music and sound into your hygge lifestyle is to find joy and contentment in the present moment. Whether you're listening to your favorite music, enjoying the sounds of nature, or simply creating a peaceful atmosphere with ambient noise, the principles of hygge can guide your choices and help you cultivate a sense of mindfulness and intentionality in your daily routine. By prioritizing relaxation, well-being, and connection through music and sound, you can promote a sense of comfort and contentment in your hygge lifestyle.

Hygge and the Art of Slow Living

Hygge is about finding joy and contentment in the simple pleasures of life, and one way to achieve this is through embracing the art of slow living. Slow living emphasizes taking the time to savor the small moments, prioritizing relaxation and well-being, and cultivating a sense of intentionality in your daily routine. In this chapter, we will explore the connection between hygge and slow living, and offer practical tips for incorporating slow living into your life.

At its core, slow living is about finding joy and contentment in the present moment, and this is central to the hygge philosophy. This might involve taking the time to savor a cup of tea, enjoying a leisurely walk, or simply taking a few moments to breathe and reflect. By prioritizing slow living in your daily routine, you can create a sense of mindfulness and intentionality that is central to the hygge philosophy.

Another way to incorporate slow living into your hygge lifestyle is through the practice of self-care and relaxation. This might involve taking a warm bath, practicing yoga, or simply taking a few moments to read a book or listen to music. By prioritizing relaxation and well-being in your daily routine, you can create a sense of comfort and contentment that is central to the hygge philosophy.

In addition to promoting relaxation and well-being, slow living can also help cultivate a sense of purpose and meaning in your daily routine. This might involve setting intentions for your day, practicing gratitude, or simply taking the time to appreciate the small moments in life. By prioritizing intentionality and mindfulness in your daily routine, you can create a sense of purpose and meaning that is central to the hygge philosophy.

Another way to incorporate slow living into your hygge lifestyle is to embrace a more minimalist and sustainable approach to life. This might involve decluttering your home, embracing a more mindful approach to consumption, or simply taking the time to appreciate the beauty of simplicity. By embracing a more minimalist and sustainable approach to life, you can create a sense of purpose and meaning that is central to the hygge philosophy.

Ultimately, the key to incorporating slow living into your hygge lifestyle is to find joy and contentment in the present moment. Whether you're taking the time to savor a cup of tea, practicing self-care and relaxation, cultivating a sense of purpose and meaning, or embracing a more minimalist and sustainable approach to life, the principles of slow living can guide your choices and help you cultivate a sense of mindfulness and intentionality in your daily routine. By prioritizing slow living and embracing the art of living in the moment, you can promote relaxation, well-being, and a sense of contentment in your hygge lifestyle.

Hygge in Travel: Embracing New Cultures with Comfort and Coziness

Hygge is about finding joy and contentment in the simple pleasures of life, and this philosophy can be applied to all aspects of life, including travel. Whether you're exploring new cultures, trying new foods, or simply taking in the sights and sounds of a new place, incorporating hygge into your travel can help promote relaxation, well-being, and a sense of comfort. In this chapter, we will explore the role of hygge in travel, and offer practical tips for incorporating comfort and coziness into your travels.

At its core, hygge is about finding joy and contentment in your surroundings, and this is central to the hygge philosophy in travel. This might involve prioritizing comfort and coziness in your accommodations, whether that means booking a cozy bed and breakfast or a luxurious hotel room with a view. By creating a sense of comfort and coziness in your accommodations, you can promote relaxation and well-being in your travels.

Another way to incorporate hygge into your travel is through the practice of slow travel. Slow travel emphasizes taking the time to truly experience a place, rather than rushing from one tourist attraction to the next. This might involve taking a leisurely walk through a new city, exploring local markets, or simply taking the time to appreciate the beauty of a new place. By prioritizing slow travel in your itinerary, you can create a sense of mindfulness and intentionality in your travels.

In addition to promoting relaxation and well-being, hygge in travel can also help promote a sense of cultural immersion and connection. This might involve trying new foods, learning about local customs and traditions, or simply taking the time to connect with locals. By prioritizing cultural immersion and connection in your travels, you can create a sense of togetherness and belonging that is central to the hygge philosophy.

Another way to incorporate hygge into your travel is to embrace a sense of adventure and exploration. This might involve trying new activities, like hiking or kayaking, or simply stepping outside of your comfort zone to try something new. By embracing a sense of adventure and exploration in your travels, you can create a sense of excitement and wonder that is central to the hygge philosophy.

Ultimately, the key to incorporating hygge into your travel is to find joy and contentment in the present moment. Whether you're prioritizing comfort and coziness in your accommodations, embracing slow travel and cultural immersion, or stepping outside of your comfort zone to try something new, the principles of hygge can guide your choices and help you cultivate a sense of mindfulness and intentionality in your travels. By prioritizing relaxation, well-being, and cultural immersion in your travels, you can promote a sense of joy and contentment that is central to the hygge philosophy.

Hygge and Self-Care: Nurturing Yourself

Hygge is all about finding joy and contentment in the simple pleasures of life, and this includes taking care of yourself. Self-care is an essential component of a hygge lifestyle, as it promotes relaxation, well-being, and a sense of comfort and coziness. In this chapter, we will explore the role of self-care in hygge, and offer practical tips for nurturing yourself in a hygge-inspired way.

At its core, self-care is about taking the time to prioritize your own well-being and happiness, and this is central to the hygge philosophy. This might involve practicing mindfulness and meditation, taking time for yourself to recharge, or simply indulging in a little bit of pampering. By prioritizing self-care in your daily routine, you can create a sense of relaxation and well-being that is central to the hygge philosophy.

Another way to incorporate self-care into your hygge lifestyle is through the practice of self-compassion. Self-compassion involves treating yourself with kindness and understanding, and recognizing that it's okay to take care of yourself, even if it means saying no to others. By practicing self-compassion in your daily routine, you can create a sense of comfort and coziness that is central to the hygge philosophy.

In addition to promoting relaxation and well-being, self-care in a hygge-inspired way can also help cultivate a sense of connection and togetherness. This might involve practicing gratitude and appreciation for the people and things in your life, or simply taking the time to connect with loved ones. By prioritizing connection and togetherness in your self-care routine, you can create a sense of belonging that is central to the hygge philosophy.

Another way to incorporate self-care into your hygge lifestyle is through the practice of mindfulness and presence. This might involve taking the time to savor a cup of tea, practice yoga or meditation, or simply taking a few moments to breathe and reflect. By practicing mindfulness and presence in your self-care routine, you can create a sense of intentionality and contentment that is central to the hygge philosophy.

Ultimately, the key to incorporating self-care into your hygge lifestyle is to find joy and contentment in nurturing yourself. Whether you're practicing mindfulness and meditation, indulging in a little bit of pampering, or simply taking the time to appreciate the small moments in life, the principles of self-care can guide your choices and help you cultivate a sense of relaxation, well-being, and comfort and coziness in your hygge lifestyle. By prioritizing self-care in a hygge-inspired way, you can promote a sense of joy and contentment that is central to the hygge philosophy.

Hygge and Mindfulness: Living in the Present Moment

Hygge is all about finding joy and contentment in the simple pleasures of life, and one of the key ways to achieve this is through the practice of mindfulness. Mindfulness is the act of being present and fully engaged in the current moment, and it is central to the hygge philosophy. In this chapter, we will explore the role of mindfulness in hygge, and offer practical tips for living in the present moment in a hygge-inspired way.

At its core, mindfulness is about being fully present and engaged in the current moment, and this is central to the hygge philosophy. This might involve practicing gratitude and appreciation for the small things in life, savoring the taste of a good meal, or simply taking the time to enjoy the beauty of nature. By prioritizing mindfulness in your daily routine, you can create a sense of intentionality and contentment that is central to the hygge philosophy.

Another way to incorporate mindfulness into your hygge lifestyle is through the practice of meditation. Meditation involves taking the time to focus your mind on the present moment, and can help promote relaxation and well-being. By incorporating meditation into your daily routine, you can create a sense of calm and peace that is central to the hygge philosophy.

In addition to promoting relaxation and well-being, mindfulness in a hygge-inspired way can also help promote a sense of connection and togetherness. This might involve practicing gratitude and appreciation for the people in your life, or simply taking the time to connect with loved ones. By prioritizing connection and togetherness in your mindfulness practice, you can create a sense of belonging that is central to the hygge philosophy.

Another way to incorporate mindfulness into your hygge lifestyle is through the practice of self-reflection. Self-reflection involves taking the time to reflect on your thoughts and feelings, and can help promote self-awareness and personal growth. By incorporating self-reflection into your daily routine, you can create a sense of intentionality and purpose that is central to the hygge philosophy.

Ultimately, the key to incorporating mindfulness into your hygge lifestyle is to find joy and contentment in living in the present moment. Whether you're practicing gratitude and appreciation, savoring the small moments in life, or simply taking the time to connect with loved ones, the principles of mindfulness can guide your choices and help you cultivate a sense of relaxation, well-being, and comfort and coziness in your hygge lifestyle. By prioritizing mindfulness in a hygge-inspired way, you can promote a sense of joy and contentment that is central to the hygge philosophy.

The Role of Hygge in Mental Health and Well-Being

Hygge is more than just a trend or a lifestyle choice – it can also play an important role in promoting mental health and well-being. By prioritizing comfort, coziness, and a sense of connection with others, hygge can help promote feelings of relaxation, contentment, and happiness. In this chapter, we will explore the role of hygge in mental health and well-being, and offer practical tips for incorporating hygge into your self-care routine.

One of the key ways that hygge can promote mental health and well-being is through its emphasis on relaxation and comfort. By creating a cozy and comfortable environment, you can promote feelings of relaxation and stress relief. This might involve curling up with a good book, lighting some candles, or simply taking the time to indulge in a little bit of pampering. By prioritizing relaxation and comfort in your daily routine, you can create a sense of peace and well-being that is central to the hygge philosophy.

Another way that hygge can promote mental health and well-being is through its emphasis on connection and togetherness. By prioritizing time with loved ones and creating a sense of community, you can promote feelings of happiness and contentment. This might involve hosting a dinner party, enjoying a game night with friends, or simply spending time connecting with loved ones. By prioritizing connection and togetherness in your daily routine, you can create a sense of belonging and support that is central to the hygge philosophy.

In addition to promoting relaxation, comfort, and connection, hygge can also help promote feelings of gratitude and appreciation. By taking the time to savor the small moments in life and practice gratitude, you can promote feelings of happiness and contentment. This might involve keeping a gratitude journal, taking the time to appreciate the beauty of nature, or simply expressing thanks for the people and things in your life. By prioritizing gratitude and appreciation in your daily routine, you can create a sense of purpose and well-being that is central to the hygge philosophy.

Another way that hygge can promote mental health and well-being is through its emphasis on self-care. By taking the time to prioritize your own well-being and happiness, you can promote feelings of self-worth and contentment. This might involve practicing mindfulness and meditation, indulging in a little bit of pampering, or simply taking the time to enjoy the simple pleasures in life. By prioritizing self-care in your daily routine, you can create a sense of relaxation and well-being that is central to the hygge philosophy.

Ultimately, the key to incorporating hygge into your self-care routine is to find joy and contentment in the small pleasures of life. Whether you're creating a cozy and comfortable environment, prioritizing time with loved ones, practicing gratitude and appreciation, or taking the time to nurture yourself, the principles of hygge can guide your choices and help you cultivate a sense of relaxation, well-being, and comfort and coziness in your daily life. By prioritizing hygge in a self-care context, you can promote a sense of joy and contentment that can help support your mental health and well-being.

Hygge and Community: Creating Connections in Your Neighborhood

Hygge is not just about creating a cozy and comfortable environment for yourself – it is also about building connections with the people around you. By prioritizing community and connection in your daily life, you can create a sense of belonging and support that is central to the hygge philosophy. In this chapter, we will explore the role of hygge in building connections in your neighborhood, and offer practical tips for fostering a sense of community in your local area.

One of the key ways to incorporate hygge into your community is by hosting gatherings and events that bring people together. This might involve organizing a neighborhood potluck, hosting a game night, or simply inviting your neighbors over for a cup of coffee. By creating opportunities for connection and togetherness, you can build a sense of community and belonging that is central to the hygge philosophy.

Another way to incorporate hygge into your community is by participating in local events and activities. Whether it's attending a farmers' market, joining a book club, or volunteering at a local charity, participating in local events and activities can help you build connections with the people around you. By prioritizing community involvement and engagement, you can build a sense of belonging and purpose that is central to the hygge philosophy.

In addition to hosting gatherings and participating in local events, another way to build connections in your neighborhood is by prioritizing kindness and generosity. This might involve performing small acts of kindness for your neighbors, such as bringing them a meal when they are sick or offering to help with yard work. By prioritizing kindness and generosity, you can build a sense of support and compassion that is central to the hygge philosophy.

Another way to incorporate hygge into your community is by embracing the outdoors and the natural environment. This might involve going for a walk in your local park, gardening in your front yard, or simply taking the time to appreciate the beauty of nature. By prioritizing a connection with the natural world, you can build a sense of appreciation and mindfulness that is central to the hygge philosophy.

Ultimately, the key to incorporating hygge into your community is to prioritize connection and togetherness. Whether you're hosting gatherings, participating in local events, practicing kindness and generosity, or embracing the natural environment, the principles of hygge can guide your choices and help you build a sense of community and belonging in your neighborhood. By prioritizing hygge in a community context, you can build connections and relationships that can help support your overall well-being and happiness.

Conclusion: Embracing Hygge as a Way of Life

Hygge is more than just a Danish concept of coziness – it is a way of life that can help us find comfort, connection, and joy in our daily lives. By embracing the principles of hygge, we can create a sense of warmth and happiness that can help us navigate the stresses and challenges of modern life. In this final chapter, we will explore how you can embrace hygge as a way of life, and offer some final thoughts on the power of hygge in today's world.

First and foremost, embracing hygge as a way of life means prioritizing comfort, coziness, and relaxation. This might involve creating a cozy reading nook in your home, taking a relaxing bath, or simply taking the time to slow down and savor a cup of tea. By prioritizing comfort and relaxation, we can help reduce stress and anxiety, and cultivate a sense of calm and contentment in our daily lives.

In addition to prioritizing comfort and relaxation, embracing hygge as a way of life means building connections with the people around us. This might involve hosting gatherings, participating in community events, or simply spending quality time with friends and loved ones. By building connections and fostering a sense of community, we can cultivate a sense of belonging and support that is central to the hygge philosophy.

Another important aspect of embracing hygge as a way of life is prioritizing simplicity and mindfulness. This might involve decluttering your home, practicing mindfulness meditation, or simply taking the time to appreciate the small moments of beauty in our daily lives. By prioritizing simplicity and mindfulness, we can cultivate a sense of gratitude and appreciation for the world around us, and find joy and contentment in the present moment.

Ultimately, embracing hygge as a way of life means prioritizing comfort, connection, and mindfulness in all aspects of our lives. Whether we are creating cozy spaces in our homes, building connections with our communities, or simply taking the time to appreciate the beauty of the world around us, the principles of hygge can guide our choices and help us find happiness and contentment in our daily lives.

In today's fast-paced and often stressful world, the principles of hygge can provide a much-needed sense of comfort and connection. By embracing hygge as a way of life, we can find joy and contentment in even the smallest moments, and cultivate a sense of warmth and happiness that can sustain us through life's challenges. So, take some time to slow down, savor the simple pleasures of life, and embrace hygge as a way of life – you may be surprised at how much it can transform your daily experience.

Thank you for taking the time to read this book on hygge. We hope that you found it insightful and inspiring, and that it has provided you with new ideas for incorporating comfort, connection, and mindfulness into your daily life.

If you enjoyed this book, we would greatly appreciate it if you could leave a positive review on your preferred platform. Your review will not only help us reach more readers, but it will also help others discover the power of hygge and its potential to bring joy and contentment into their lives.

Thank you again for your support, and we hope that you continue to embrace the principles of hygge as a way of life.

Printed in Great Britain
by Amazon

34919426R00030